Come
to
Mount Shasta

Sacred Path Poetry

Come To Mount Shasta

Sacred Path Poetry

Some of the poems in this collection first appeared in Know Your Way, Love Unconditional, and Follow the White Rabbit chapbooks; and on facebook.

Cover credit, photo taken by Catherine Preus, 2023.

First edition.

Published by Four Wild Geese Design, Mount Shasta, California 96067

ISBN 978-1-7324373-9-5

Preface

A famous quote describing Mount Shasta is "Where heaven meets earth". Out of the many sacred, powerful sites on Earth, Mt. Shasta holds the distinction of being elevating and grounding at the same time. It is said she is both the crown chakra and the root chakra of the Earth.
Quite a distinction.

Mt. Shasta is also referred to by many as Mama Shasta. She is a divine feminine being looking over us.

Mountains are high places, both physically and energetically. Higher frequencies support the gathering of higher beings such as ascended masters, the Telosians and star family that visit Earth.

People are called to come to Mount Shasta either to visit or stay on. Those who listen are blessed with unique experiences tailored to their needs. Some of those experiences and perspectives are shared here. Contributors keep all rights to their work. Gratitude for the sharing.

"Expansion from limited earth drama to places of source in the ethers, the cloud places where energies originate." Darrel Johannes

"With philosophy
He contemplates the mountain...
Old professor frog."   ISSA

Many thanks to these contributors:

Catherine Preus

Yeshardo

Michelle Berditschevsky

Christine O'Brien

A'Marie B. Thomas-Brown

Jennifer Hershelman

Joa Janakoayas

Darrel Johannes

Maria Lodes

Cody Ray Richardson

Rita Chambers

Joseph Alves

Omanasa Star

Contents

Come to Mount Shasta by Cheryl

Come to Mount Shasta,
the docking port,
and dock your ship.

Experience sacred time.
Flow in the headwaters.

Know your mission.
Read your book of life.
Walk your sacred path.

See the way of Life, Love and Learning.

Keep planting the trees of Life.
Assist those on their path.

Be the Open Door,
Connect, Support, Strengthen.

Accept Divine Possibilities.

For Shasta through Yeshardo

With reflective sunset snow
And lenticular halo
A sweet splendor to behold
Ancient, but you don't get old!

Some folks call you a portal
An interdimensional hub
Your firry forrests fertile
Abounding with good-ass grub

Is it true you're a chakra?
Is it crown or is it root?
That's cool if you're a chakra!
And a volcano to boot!

Thanks for not erupting lately
Suppressing age old gasses
Your posture remains stately
A beacon for the masses

Gateway to earth so hollow
Containing city Telos
Show us in and we'll follow
Meeting tall, blue-ish fellows

Attracting hippies and freaks
Buddhists, rawfoodists, and Sikhs
Purveyors of crystal, not meth
Breatharians circumvent death

In circular formations
Ascended masters percuss
Archangels work the gas stations
With esoteric stuff to discuss

Throbbing orbs traverse night skies
Gaping mouths, quivering lips
There's no need to check your eyes
You just saw fucking spaceships!

Sweet psychedelic snowcone!
Glistening dew, shimmering light
From your pores forge gemstones
Magical, shiny, and bright
2

Paved upon with modern roads
Punctured by the power poles
And still you send us the codes
Casting us upon our roles

A sacred space for chipmunks
Manzanitas, bears, and shrooms
So rife with such enrichments
And kaleidoscopic blooms

So thank you Mama Shasta
And all celestial fam
Convergence has been a blast-a
And It can't be sold by the gram

Hawk encounter
by Michelle Berditschevsky

traveling home on the conifer-lined road
between Burney and Mount Shasta
I slowed for a little furry animal, a rabbit
crossing both lanes ahead of me

just as I braked
hawk saw rabbit and swooped down
windshield shattered slivers in my lap
bird flopped on pavement
like a crumpled brown cloth

even lifeless, it emanated a wild power
          and I knelt as if I'd been told
to pick up and lay the limp feathers softly
to rest in its forest home

home was a silence that spread
into the canopy and covered
every rock, every needle and cone
the entire forest floor
with a gaze of lingering gold
in the primal layer of the world

and I learned
another stratum of self, a silent song
of my new name disguised
as hawk

giving wing even to sorrow
woven into the fabric of the world

Mountain passage
by Michelle Berditschevsky

*first find the tree by the path that lets
you in
and the large rock that is the portal
there's one on every trail, stop there and
feel
the true place where she lives*

> *at the base is a way of seeing and
> listening
> to breathe in silence with the
> forest
> until a tone responds
> from the Oneness within all life...*

*high on the Mountain in early light
from deep in the night a long pure note
spreads the symphony of dawn
light and sky impose their presence*

> *breathe in dark trunk
> breathe out swaying branches
> breathe in glistening needles*

*breathe out in all directions
roots deep, arms reaching high
grounding the spark of an unseen source*

> *this...is the face of an ancient
> thought
> etched in our cells, a primordial
> future
> toward which we are groping...*

*this fierce love like a stream winds a path
around obstacles, among the eddies
and byways of the human drama*

> *inserting itself as a wild player*

> *an emissary of all that is untamed
> and giving
> reminding us...
> that our survival depends on it*

The Spirit of All Life

by Catherine Preus

It is so hard to live,
to know how to live in a sacred manner
Darkness and confusion reign
but underneath it all
the spirit of All Life
moves and breaks through in terrible
and wonderful truth

It is so hard to live
We are a scattered and broken people
set adrift, looking for crumbs.

Once, the whole of life was strong,
people knew how to live.
Daily life was good,
organized along sacred lines
like the bees and the ants.
People knew their sacred role.
The way was clear,
revealed to all through visions
and prayers that were the
invisible ropes that guided and
helped all on the daily path of living.

To be alive
was not so hard
as it is today
with every person alone,
each day striving to hold the faith.

For to live without the collective agreement
it is harder,
much harder,
to know how to live,
how to learn,
how to worship.

Life becomes chaotic and dark
people bicker and fight amongst themselves
only a few people survive,
living what's real in their hearts.
The poets and artists feel this the most.
Others cling desperately to their illusions of happiness.
Drink and despair and insanity flow through humanity
like a dark current sweeping
many into the gutter.

But a New Day is coming!
A New Day is here!

So it is said,
and I believe it.

We can only share our brokenness
and thus help, by healing our own wounds,
to make this new day possible,
this day which is dawning
with a terrible and wonderful
certainty, and which like the sun,
can no longer be held back.

New ways are blending with old ways
so that the prayers are once again being said,
and shared vision will once again guide us.

This time of trouble, this darkness
which at times, seems even to blot out
the golden sun's light,
will end
as the Christ Spirit and Divine Mother
awaken in our hearts,
and the Sun's golden rays stream out
to bathe and infuse all of us
and everything with light!

Observation on a Buddha Rock
by Christine O'Brien

I know loneliness
a rock separated from a streambed
my particular glamour
is less appealing here.
Like this displaced rock
am I commonplace
or too old?

This rock, a misshapen Buddha
solitary Bodhisattva
witnessing the cleaving
remembering the whole.

What dissension shattered humankind
into *separation*?
Lonely and separate as this scarred rock
perhaps once praised for its cool detachment.
Who cares to decipher the untold encrypted story?

A star has fallen
to the bottom of the sea
fossilized
while a starfish rises
in the darkening sky
alternating realities.

God is in us--
is all right with the world?
Has the rock learned compassion?
Is that the panacea for loneliness?

Posted Like a Daffodil
by A'Marie B. Thomas-Brown

Posted like a daffodil on a sunny day
Running like a faucet
Like children at play
Listening to the stillness
As we climb the limbs and boughs
Carrying sunshine in us
From crowns to tippy toes
Laughing as if no tomorrow
Can parlay in the now of today
Crystalline brings in flesh suits
Cultivating happiness pursuits
In our hearts
In our minds
In our beingness
I digress
Words have the power
That we embody
ITs essence
We breathe
We be
Entirely
Off to the cornfields we go
Harvesting what we sow
In tears
In love
IN Light
Take flight
Soaring beyond galaxies
And black holes
One soul
One mind
One Spirit
This is it
Poetically
Rhythmically
Ethereally
Sound

Posted like a daffodil ✿
On this sunny day

Fill Your Vase
by Cheryl

Ticking sounds behind me.
Clock.
Mix of cold and warm air.
Artificial fire.

Spring brings vibrant colours---
Red, Yellow and Green.

But my favorite are the trees pink with blossoms.

Crocuses poking their heads up
thru their dirt blanket.

A circle of daffodils.

Some flowers volunteer their life
to join us in our homes--

But the happiest ones
are stretching their roots,
dancing in the wind,
basking in the sun.

White Rabbit
by Cheryl

I live in a flat--
it is my castle.

The Grandmother Pine
stands guard--

I follow the steps of my brothers
White Brotherhood--
their guidance keeps me in the light.

I am white lunar wind.

White Buffalo Calf woman is a sister--
also the albino squirrel who played in the park
that summer day.

I am White Lily--
a white dove.

The white rose is my sister--
so many plants in my room.
They are glad to see me when
I come home.

I become the white rabbit.

The white rabbit appears as a sign that life will be all the more beautiful from here. It is also an interpretation that you will begin new chapters in your life. The animal kingdom reminds you at this time that however you see yourself...the world will follow your lead. Know that you are safe and protected and loved deeply. Do not fear the changes you are making dear one. The rabbit reminds you to step forward through your fears, and you will experience the mystical aspects of life even more.

Faith by Christine O'Brien

When the not-so-far ridges have been obscured
by smoke for months...
When your mind is clouded with confusing thoughts...
When what you once perceived proves to be false
or limiting...
When you sip your morning
cup of tea and place one foot
in front of the other
and say yes to this new day,
you have learned faith.

The smoke hangs on the ridge waiting for
directions from the wind.
The firefighters are out there
day and night manning
bulldozers, helicopters, heavy machinery--
we trust them to do their jobs--
to be wisely directed by those
who understand the nature
of fighting fire in a heavily forested area
with up and down rugged terrain. We
have to trust them. We have to trust
and to hold onto faith that everything is
going to be alright...
and until then,
that we can bear it--
be strong
be patient
and live our lives truly
and boldly. We have to trust that we have
sufficient courage,
to share our gifts and
to proceed
into this new day.
We go forward into the uncertainty
on wings of prayer, hope and trust
and faith
and whatever love looks like today.
Then, I go into the garden to harvest tomatillos.

Replenishing by Jennifer H.

Sitting silent in the woods
a gentle breeze brushes by your face
its not the wind
the trees are breathing all around you

Breathing life into the world,
       Replenishing

Standing, silently, crying against a trunk
-sweet release, ease the energy out

Trees

Soaking in your tears, your fears
Holding space for all your pain
with nothing to gain

But a song, of love and gratitude
       Replenishing
Necessary.

For the space they hold
for us all

Standing tall
beacons of energy

Anchoring in reality

Shifting the winds

Swirling the world
into
Peace and balance.

Becoming by Joa Janakoayas

From the dirty bowels
Of the earth mother
After a long winters sleep
Daring to leave behind the
Unconscious underworld
Is aroused in the warm sunshine
A meek green shoot
Clean and shiny
Yawning and stretching
Secretly moving
Magically expanding
Urgently becoming
Naked to all
Crushed if unnoticed
Eaten if found
The meek sprout sends down
One white hairy projection
To support the quest for light.
For maturity
Two unfolding infantile leaflets
With big plans!

Belonging by Joa Janakoayas

All my life I have been longing
For a more true feeling of belonging

Today I found the answer
That divine anchor

that makes everything right
so I can give up the mental fight

The answer was beneath my feet all along
It is Mother Earth that makes me strong

She takes away all my fears
And her love moves me to tears

reminding me all is well
Her flowers have me in a happy spell

Thank you Mother Earth - I love you so
May my steps be more conscious and slow

To be aware of every miracle
You make beautifully visual.

On you I drop to my knees
Underneath your blowing trees

In rapture of your aliveness
Expanding my heart to the giant US!
Now I can feel safe in our Oneness.

I Want a New Me by Darrel Johannes

Day after day, year after year
the same old me, I wish I would disappear.

The same old thoughts, actions and deeds--
Oh, how I wish I could just be freed.

I often catch a glimpse of the horizon,
the place where what I have been meets eternity.

Could I really leave it, all I have known
and run with fervor to my authentic home.

The place where all misery, strife and pain
would vanish, to less than a memory on a forgotten plain.

I have started my journey, but the price is high
with the only alternative being left to die.

The path is a bit varied for each, I suppose
but the door to our past we all must close.

Life is only here, now in this breath
to ruminate on what was, is certain death.

Our life is made new if we accept the seasons--
Its a miracle of sorts and defies all reason.

Categories kill-- they diminish the mystery.
Our presence is more than facts, logic and history.

Lets catch a wave, take a breath,
allow the spirit its life, in abandon--
Be still, move on, get cleansed
and you will hear it.

Sanctuary by Darrel Johannes

The road to Church is full of feelings,
times of loneliness, times of healing.

Sometimes expecting more than it is
leaves me empty, feeling amiss.

Seeking a refuge from cruelty and shame,
but often there I feel the same.

Challenges and guidelines, the way explained
when all I need is simple refrain.

Refrain from study, logic and plans--
only desiring to rest safe in his hands.

Hands that hold, heal and bless
Removed from the world's mechanical mess.

The competition is there to show what we know--
the pressure is on to "grow grow grow".

Pressure cooked to perfection, where's the good in that?
Presto Saint--right out of the hat.

Good growth is slow, deliberate and right.
We yield to the spirit and give up the fight.

We fight and demand to know how it works--
Dear God please deliver us from arrogance.

Sanctuary, just the sound draws me in--
a place of mercy, compassion and kin.

A place of safety from the world's ways
a place to be just me, free from the craze.

From the craze of performance, judgment and stress
to a place of warmth, beauty and rest.

Sanctuary, not a building, address or place--
its an attitude we build with forgiveness, acceptance, and grace.

At Dawn
by Maria Lodes

Returning to Wholeness
    —early morning
Eyes open
    —focus Within

Seeing the world
    through an Inner Eye—
Door opens wide
    —glorious the View

Quiet and peaceful
    —filled with Love
A taste of Reality
    —Who I Am

World transforms
    —wondrous to me
Me who has shrunk back
    —a witness at most

A place of Knowing
    —impermanence
Wanting to stay
    —where wanting is taboo

A demanding world
    pulls me back—
It comes with amnesia
    —forgot who I Am

The vision a Gift
    —will return again
Cleansing old habits
    rigid ways of the mind...

Left behind
    a glimpse of sun Light
Glancing off dawn's
    precious dewdrops...

18

Faery Falls
by Maria Lodes

Time of Movement
        —disrupts old patterns
Frozen parts awaken
        —return to Source

Warm Spring winds
        stirred by Nature—
Melt quickly the ice
        transform the snow—

Myriads of channels
        simultaneously fill—
Turbulent waters
        Converge as One—

Gathering force
        —cliff's vulnerable edge
With a boundless leap
        fills the basin below—

Paused a Moment
        —a swirling current
It rushes on over boulders
        —its destination pursuing...

Recognizing Change
        —impermanent by nature
Trusting Within
        —resistance subsides..

Preserved
by Cheryl

I'm
Reserved--
Safe.
My constraints are comforting,
loose fitting.

I peek around the corner,
observing all--
Preserved--
moments in time--
snapshots--
saved in space.

Giving meaning to the moment,
making it eternal.

Footprints in the quantum field--
Preserved.

Hush
by Cheryl

Dawn murmurs
through the tranquil mist--

Hush, and you will hear her golden melody.

Feel the luminous rays.

The slyphs are waking,
Hush--

murmurs become messages--
decipher the unintelligible--

Know the tranquil tone
of peace.

The original natural way
comes with every
Grand Rising--
Pulling the curtain
to another day.

Council Meeting
by Cheryl

Council of nine---
Don't be in a hurry--
Be here, Now--
in this moment.

Galactic guidance--
Will you listen? Tune in.
A clear vessel, has no leaks,
secure in your knowing.
(your report is here)

This is not a test, it is real.
Your assignment--should you choose
to accept it.
Your key--your code--mystery solved,
final puzzle piece.

epigee (apogee)
by Cheryl

I am a bud, gradually gently opening.

Nothing will come to pass
if it doesn't receive your energy.

Illusions dissipate without our(creator) energy.

"You are generating this hologram beloved,"

It doesn't matter
What
they are doing.

Just
Walk away--
Like
An epigee of awareness--
You can
love all from a distance.

Day 11
by A'Marie B. Thomas-Brown

Eleven, a number of
Transition
Transformation
And Temperance

Remembrance

Labor and Delivery
Conception, zygote, seed
A new breed

Conscious creative beings
11 -in number
It will wear off
Yet its impact remains

Two singles or a double
Depending on the perspective
The spiritual bubble
Ethereal Hubble

Reminiscent of all that glitters
Birds flitter
Eyes flutter
We utter

Shifting frequencies and paradigms
Universality and Cosmos
Holy Ghost
Great Spirit
Mother Earth
Father Sky

This is the 11th Hour
by Cheryl

Following the sacred path to Mount Shasta--
The Man who fell to Earth,
I didn't just fall--
I dove.

This is a sirius(serious) mission.
Sirius, blue star(25 times brighter),
Like a big brother to our sun,
Dogstar--
a faithful dog guiding his hunter,
Leading the Way.
Earth will find her way home.
This is the 11th hour.

Dance by Jennifer H.

When the earth was new
the plants had barely grown
no medicine was known

people needed healing

sisters sat in council
and felt into their hearts
where a primal energy swirled

just as the winds that cross
the plains, bringing in the rain

When they stood together and
stretched their bodies out
the Earth shifted beneath their feet

helping them to feel complete
as they continued stretching
and twirling in the dirt

their hearts overflowed
primal healing rushing
from head to toe

Each movement affecting a change
within the others...
with their hearts beating in harmony
their bodies moving to the rhythm
of their stomping feet, in sync
with the breath of the Earth

The clouds began to swim and shift
with them, the sisters
twist and flow
as rain poured down
the dirt turned to mud

the healing energy,
a giant wave--

26

Dance as a healing art
was born that day,
a sacred and ancient gift
from the spirits
that is most powerful
when it comes from the heart--
not to be misused to get your way
not to be abused, to lie, cheat and confuse.

It's time.
Come back to the start,
feel it from your heart,
time to hold space for
healing to take place.

Oil & Water by Cheryl

Imagine a reality where the trees talk to you---
The giving tree---
Its said "You get what you give".

A New world---
where all is shared---afterall,
everything we have is a gift from the universe.

My learning will be
primal, natural, eternal.
The forest is my guru.

Look to the elders---
they carry wisdom bundles---
like a cord of wood--
Do they charge a special price---
$144 for a bundle?

The teachings are clear--
like water--
The cost or fee is like oil---
not clean.
Clouds up the clear.
Oil and water don't mix.

Church and State.
Step away from the matrix.

The sacred way has all but become polluted with commerce---
It is not needed.
There is another way.

Physical cost is for physical things.
Sacred things are a gift.

Ask your ancestors---
talk to the masters--
how to move into the new
5D Earth?

Live a new way
by
remembering the old ways.

Let go of the belief--
there must be a gift for a gift--
Become light as a feather
in your giving.
The exchange will be your freedom.

What holds you back keeps
this reality in place.
What are you holding onto?

The indigenous know
not to charge
for what is sacred.

Our ancestors are waiting for us---
give up the bone.

Be open to new ways
of doing, thinking, and living.
Ask yourself--
What is the next best step?
Do that.
Step by step--
we gain our
freedom and victory!

Ancient by Jennifer H.

Singing to the tree--
the words, ancient and deep
from another time,
nearly forgotten, hidden, asleep.

Suddenly,
everything shifts, merges and converges.

Now,
I'm sitting in the tree,
feeling it become me.
When I open my eyes,
I'm touching the sky
The wind blowing through me as leaves on the tree
totally and utterly free.

I flow to the ground
traveling through roots
reaching out,
as far as the eye can see--
energy all connected, intertwined and integrated.

The black hills grass giggled and tickled above
as I flow through roots below.

I feel the wind again,
russling and tussling
as the Buffalo I saw a mile back
now,
stands over and on me.
Grass is a hive mind,
each blade blows singularily and together.
They giggle harmoniously.
The wind tickled
as we giggled and waved
loving to be swayed.

For a brief moment,
I feel myself rise
and see through Buffalo eyes.

Then snap,
I'm back at the tree
feeling my body, all around me
my feet planted in dirt.
Standing in sunshine,
bees singing to me.

Now,
time to move along.
Nothing can go wrong.
Time to help people live,
pure, connected and free.

Matter by Cody Ray Richardson

Thought proceeds matter
Your matter is forming around us
For us
By us
We care
Be careful
Be full
Care
Rainbow bright
Your bright
Light
Frequency

The Mountain
by Cody Ray Richardson

The mountain takes me
Magnifying what's within
She breaks me
Only I can make me whole again
This magnificent magnifier
Truth unraveled
Tumbled in desire
So long my soul has traveled
Hear her singing like a choir
Her frequency is changing me
Like fresh attire
Shifting my reality
Some of my shoes have outlasted
my many relationship so far
The more I reach out for something to hold on
The more moments slip by and are gone
It's easy when I let go
It's so difficult to uphold
A reality that does not value me
Oh how but I do value my heart of gold
I love myself enough to make it Through
Another unfolding of my shadow
I'm a gem inside
Shining through the dark Night of my soul
I met the devil at the cross roads
Just the other night
He told a future before it happened
As if he had future sight
Just because they make it work
Does not make it right
So watch out for the mutants
They will take your light at night
Keep your closest friends really close
In these hardened times
Freedom is a daily choice
And a bit of a daily grind
There may be rough waters ahead
So choose your crew well captain
We will travel throughout this land
To uphold a dream to hold her hand
for the first time again

What is a date?

Little short visits, where two people behave their best.

Wanna get to know someone?
Do business with them--
over and over again,
then you will see their true self,
really get to know them.

Hope Is a Deep Well

Joy of a soaring bird--
Peace of a day off--
A well deserved rest.

Ficus Tree

Leaves gently swaying.
Ficus Tree, in bedroom--
Reaches for ceiling.

The train bellows--
I'm coming--
Watch out--
Stand back.

In Winter--

Grandmother squirrel
slides on snow covered branches.
The cat plays with yarn.

I wonder why the bluebird sings--
A call for love, long lost.
Poets long dead await
our words, our hopes, our dreams.

34

Stellar Jays
by Cheryl

Kin to the Crow--
the Elite of their family.
All dressed up for their weekly Luncheon.

The jays hold council,
they gather at the city park---

Very observant,
watching all who go by---

Sometimes they talk to me.

Dedicated to my friend Brother Blue Jay.

Far Off Worlds
by Rita Chambers

We do come from
    far off worlds,
With joys, griefs
    and longings.
We are like prayers
    in search
of the one who prays.

Come Sit With Me
by Joseph Alves

Blue sky, white clouds and trees,
it's really healing and calming.
Your life is my dream.

Cutting Through
by Maria Lodes

Cutting through illusion
   —veil of deception
Allows What Is
   —To Be in the Moment...

That's all there Is
   —this One Moment
Unchanging
   Permanent...

My Place by Darrel Johannes

Expansion from limited earth drama to places of source in the
ethers, the cloud places where energies originate.

It will all drop off with such ease,
the small limited being I wrongly came to believe I am.

There is nothing to miss here when the scope of my essence,
my rightful place
in the theme of the universe is understood and loved.

There is nothing to miss about confusion,
limitation and error.

I will know
just as
I will be known.

My Prayer by Jennifer H.

My Wish

is for peace, love, balance,

freedom and unhindered healing for all;

the land, the water, the spirits,

all beings and people.

Thank-You

My Will / Thy Will
What is a love offering?
by Omanasa Star

I prayed for many years the Lords Prayer--"Thy will be done on earth as it is in heaven" without knowing what "Thy will" was. Yet often wondering.

It's the still small voice within, some one told me. Well, it took me years of listening and of many dynamic meditations before I became aware that my mind had to become still so that I could listen to my heart. And yes there was indeed a still, small voice. Still, like the sound of falling snow, small like a newborn child and it grew like flowers grow, so non-
intrusive, so delicate, yielding to the slightest breeze of my mind trying to keep "my will" in charge. It took many years of practicing and listening to my heart's song. How did I practice?:
I started asking:
> What am I to do?
> Where am I to go?
> What am I to give?

I would only tell a chosen few about that practice. I was laughed at enough. Then meditating was out, now it is HALLELUYA IN!

It was 1982 at Unity Church in Walnut Creek that I asked every time the basket came around, "what am I to give?". My will said, "a dollar, you have only $20 left for the rest of the month". Thy will said "$3". My will screamed "$3, your nuts!".

Next Sunday came around. "What am I to give?" I asked. (I had $10 left and no clue where or when the next income opportunity would manifest) "$7", said the still small voice. I almost listened to my outraged mind with all it's good reasons. (The mind, ego, is a frightened child). I was almost in tears when I put $7 in the basket. When I came home my daughter told me someone had called for a massage. My first client. Halleluya. I asked for $40. He gave me $70. I allowed my tears to gently rinse out the fear of survival.

Next Sunday came around. I had $60 and was in a spending mood, nevertheless I asked.
I heard:
> "NOTHING"   WHAT??
> "NOTHING"   WHY???
> "NOTHING"

"Well OK" I said, doubting but willing to obey. "This makes no sense" said my will, "you should be ashamed". And ashamed I was. The basket got passed: "Please, just a quarter so others don't think...or do think..."NOTHING" was the response from deep within.

I left the church quickly, no socializing today. I felt, as if all the eyes that had seen me put NOTHING in the basket followed me and I felt like a thief. In my car I let the "thief" cry and my reasoning mind got swept into the great silence and I heard and I knew:

TO THYN OWN SELF BE TRUE

Perceptions
by Unknown Author

meet strangers,
call them experiences.
make friends,
call them mirrors.

      entangle with lovers,
      call them reflections.
      call in soul mates
      and call them awareness.

           embrace enemies,
           call them lessons.
           invite teachers,
           call them medicine.

Author page--

Cheryl Lunar Wind lives in the Mount Shasta area in a little town
called Weed. She is a practicer of Mayan cosmology, Lakota
ceremony, Star Knowledge and the Universal Laws including the
Law of One. Her hobbies are writing poetry, music, dance,
drum circles and love for all life; plant, animal and crystal. Cheryl
has been a guide and spiritual teacher for many years. Now she
shares wisdom and wit through poetry, and has published poetry
books; Know Your Way, We Are One, Follow the White Rabbit,
Love Your Light, LIFE: Shared thru Poetry, Come to Mount Shasta:
Sacred Path Poetry and co-authored We Are Forever: Awaken With
Poetry.

Testimonials---

"Cheryl's poetry is very inspiring--particularly the way she compares
life with the forces of nature. There is a special element in her
poems that opens my heart and fills my soul with divine
possiblities."
Giovanna Taormina, Co-Founder, One Circle Foundation

"Cheryl's poems have helped me to uncover and honor my own
hidden memories. The beauty of her spirit is evident in each tender,
insightful passage."
Marguerite Lorimer, www.earthalive.com

"A rare collection filled with raw, courageous honesty. Thought
provoking words that will stop you in your tracks."
Snow Thorner, ED Open Sky Gallery, Montague, California

"When wisdom, guidance, confirming comfort, ect. arrives to us
humans--from beings with the perspective of other realms--it is a
divine gift. Especially in the form of what we call poetry, and
through a being with no agenda; Cheryl Lunar Wind simply shares
what source gives her!"
--Dragon Love (Thomas) Budde

Made in the USA
Monee, IL
02 October 2023